Grolier Enterprises Inc. offers a varied selection of both
adult and children's book racks. For details on ordering
please write: Grolier Enterprises Inc., Sherman Turnpike,
Danbury, CT 06810 Attn: Premium Department

NOW YOU CAN READ....
A CURE FOR NAAMAN

STORY RETOLD BY LEONARD MATTHEWS

ILLUSTRATED BY JOHN JAMES

Library of Congress Cataloging in Publication Data

Matthews, Leonard.
    A cure for Naaman.

    (Now you can read—Bible stories)
    Summary: Retells the Bible story of Naaman, a
wealthy man who was cured of leprosy by the prophet
Elisha.
    1. Naaman, the Syrian—Juvenile literature.
2. Bible.   O.T.—Biography—Juvenile literature.
3. Bible stories, English—O.T.   Kings, 2nd.
[1. Naaman, the Syrian.   2. Elisha, the prophet.
3. Bible stories—O.T.]   I. Title.   II. Series.
BS580.N2M38   1984   222'.54'0924   [B]   84-15131
ISBN 0-86625-309-2

GROLIER ENTERPRISES CORP.

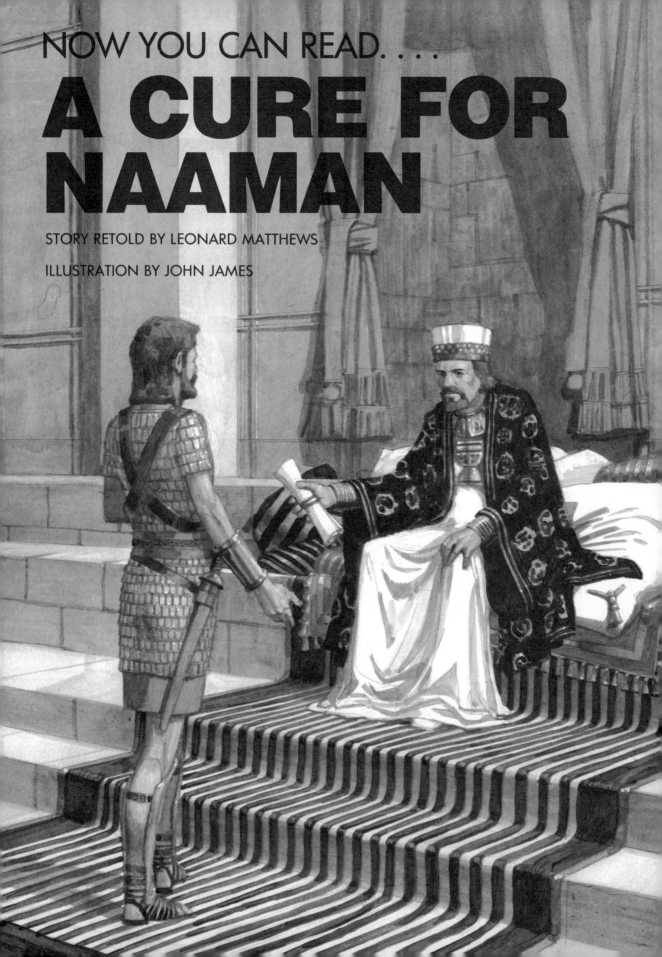

NOW YOU CAN READ.....
A CURE FOR NAAMAN

STORY RETOLD BY LEONARD MATTHEWS

ILLUSTRATION BY JOHN JAMES

Long ago there lived a man who believed in God. His name was Elisha. He lived in Israel. He did many wonderful things. One day a poor widow came to him. She owed a lot of money. She could not pay. By law she would have to sell her two sons as slaves to pay the money she owed. Broken hearted, she went to Elisha.

"What do you have of value at home?" he asked her.

"Nothing except a pot of olive oil," replied the poor woman.

"Go and borrow from your neighbors all the pots they can loan you," said Elisha.

The widow wondered at this.

"Lock your door," said Elisha. "Let nobody in. Pour oil from your pot into the pots you have borrowed."

The widow went away. She did what Elisha had told her to do.

Later she went to look at the pots. Every one was full of oil.

It could only have been God who did this. She sold the oil. She had enough money to pay the debt she owed.

The fame of Elisha spread far and wide. When he brought a dead boy to life, all Israel spoke about him.

Now, to the north of Israel lay the land of Syria. The King of Syria was named Ben-hadad. During his reign Israel and Syria fought twice.

The leader of Ben-hadad's armies was a general called Naaman. He was a very brave soldier. The king liked him. He was rich. He was happily married. There was no reason why he should not enjoy life.

Then, suddenly, something happened to end Naaman's happiness. He fell ill with leprosy. This was a terrible disease. It could not be cured.

What could Naaman do? A little girl from Israel had an answer to the question.

Some time before she had been captured by some of Naaman's soldiers. Now she was working as a servant in his house. She went to the wife of Naaman.

"I know how the master can be cured," she said.

The little girl told Naaman's wife all about Elisha. "I know Elisha could cure the master," she said. When King Ben-hadad learned about the little girl, he sent for Naaman.

"You must go to Israel and ask this wonderful man Elisha to cure you," said the king. "I will write a letter for you. Give it to Joram, the King of Israel."

So, Naaman went to Israel. He took with him a lot of gold and silver.

Naaman did not know where he could find Elisha. He went to King Joram. He gave him Ben-hadad's letter. Ben-hadad had thought that the great man Elisha was living at Joram's court. That was not so.

Joram read Ben-hadad's letter:
"I have sent Naaman to you so that you can cure him of leprosy."
Joram did not know what to do.
He did not know how to cure leprosy.
He was afraid.
Was Ben-hadad trying to start a war with him?

News of Ben-hadad's letter soon reached Elisha. He smiled to himself. He wrote to Joram.

His letter read: "Tell Naaman to wash in the River Jordan seven times. He will be cured."

When Naaman
heard this, he
was very angry.
Why the River
Jordan?
What was wrong
with the rivers
of Syria?

His friends knew
that he did not
understand things
clearly when he
was angry.
"Elisha is not
asking you to do
very much.
Why not do
as he says?"
they said.

At last Naaman agreed. He rode in his beautiful chariot. He drove to the River Jordan.

Slowly, he stepped into the river. He did this seven times. Then he looked at himself.

Wonder of wonders! The leprosy had disappeared. When he first dipped his body in the water it had been sickly white. Now it was a healthy pink. "I have been cured by Elisha's God," he said as he dressed himself. He drove to Elisha's house.

He thanked Elisha again and again. Then he offered Elisha the gold and silver he had brought. Elisha would not take it. "Why should you pay me?" asked Elisha.

"It was not I who cured you. It was my God."

Naaman was very surprised when Elisha said this. He thought for a few moments. Then he smiled. "I understand," replied Naaman. "I have learned today that your God is the only true God." He went back to Syria but, from that day on, he worshipped Elisha's God.

All these appear in the pages of the story. Can you find them?

Naaman

little girl
from Israel

Naaman's
wife

King Ben-hadad

King Joram

Elisha

messenger boy

Naaman's chariot

Now tell the story in your own words.